Accursed
Poets

Accursed Poets

Dissident Poetry from Soviet Russia 1960–1980

Edited and translated
by Anatoly Kudryavitsky

Smokestack Books
1 Lake Terrace, Grewelthorpe, Ripon HG4 3BU
e-mail: info@smokestack-books.co.uk
www.smokestack-books.co.uk

ISBN 9781916139299

Smokestack Books
is represented
by Inpress Ltd

This book has been selected to receive financial assistance from English PEN's "PEN Translates" programme, supported by Arts Council England. English PEN exists to promote literature and our understanding of it, to uphold writers' freedoms around the world, to campaign against the persecution and imprisonment of writers for stating their views, and to promote the friendly co-operation of writers and the free exchange of ideas. www.englishpen.org

Содержание

Contents

Introduction

Western readers are well acquainted with poetry written in Russia over the last three centuries, from Alexander Pushkin to Anna Akhmatova, mostly through translations. Some other Russian poets, including Vladimir Nabokov and Joseph Brodsky, felt at home at writing in English. This book offers an opportunity to hear a few 'other,' less familiar voices.

As Vladimir Nabokov once put it, 'Literature belongs to the department of specific words and images rather than to the department of general ideas.' Unfortunately, the general idea in Communist Russia was to encourage and publish only those writers who supported and even glorified the regime. It was Government policy, especially strict after the last world war. It is inconceivable now that any European poet could write a paean for the President of the European Council, but we have to bear in mind that in Communist Russia, even in the 1980s, this sort of poetry was a commonplace. Other poets ran the risk of being treated with suspicion by each and every literary vigilante. Should we be surprised by Marina Tsvetayeva's line: 'All the poets are Jews'?

In late 1930s, political trials were conducted in secret and in the absence of defence attorneys; those kangaroo courts sent a few million people to their deaths in KGB execution cellars and Siberian labour camps. During the next generation's lifetime, the secrecy of repressions was challenged by the dissidents who tried to document the Soviet regime's atrocities and to make the outside world aware of them. A number of poets were involved in dissident activities, and some of them served a prison term because of that. Yuri Galanskov, a poet, historian, human-rights activist and dissident, edited the samizdat almanac *Phoenix*; for that, he was incarcerated in prisons and labour camps, and also had to endure forced treatment in psychiatric hospitals, in one of which he died. Yuli Daniel too was a political prisoner, and in 1966 was tried along with another writer, Andrey Sinyavsky; both were convicted of anti-Soviet propaganda solely because of their literary work: for publishing their satirical writings abroad. Yuri Aikhenvald was arrested several times and forcibly held in a psychiatric institution.

Grigory Podyapolsky was a member of the unofficial human-rights committee founded by Andrei Sakharov, a Nobel Peace Prize winner, in 1971; soon after that he was summoned by the Soviet secret police and made to undergo a psychiatric examination. Victor Nekipelov spent nine years in prison for his participation in the Moscow Helsinki Group, one of Russia's leading human-rights organisations. Natalia Gorbanevskaya took part in the 1968 Red Square demonstration against the Soviet invasion of Czechoslovakia. In 1970, a Soviet court sentenced her to incarceration in a psychiatric hospital. She was released in 1972, and emigrated from the USSR in 1975, settling in France. Kari Unksova, the editor of a unofficial feminist almanac, was arrested several times and finally killed in an accident involving a KGB surveillance car. No wonder that another dissident, Natalia Gorbanevskaya, had a recurring nightmare about 'a black car pursuing her and bordering the pavement,' as she described it in one of her poems. That was the harsh reality and the danger Russian dissidents were facing daily.

In these circumstances some Russian poets chose to refrain from publishing anything openly, while others were banned from publishing. Writing 'into the drawers' became customary for them. Many of them explored the possibilities of so-called 'open poetry'. Some of them forged a radical new poetic, reconsidering writing techniques and language itself. By stripping their pieces down to a most basic expression, and outlawing most literary devices or even emotional colouring, they focused their attention on individual words or even on fragments of those words and sound units from them. This style was later defined as minimalism. One can trace the sources of modern-day minimalist texts to Dadaist, Surrealist, Concrete and even Zen poetry, and it definitely displays parallels to the visual arts. Minimalist poets focused on bare words or phrases, sometimes rearranging them on the page so that their most basic and individual properties disclosed something unexpected about themselves.

There were also predominantly minimalist Moscow poets, e.g. Ian Satunovsky who was keen on exploring the possibilities of incorporating direct speech in his texts. Similarly to Vsevolod Nekrasov, he succeeded in dismantling traditional forms of irony and understatement. Satunovsky and another Moscow poet of the 1970s, Mikhail Sokovnin, who wrote lyrical miniatures, as well as *predmetniki*, i.e. object-based poems, saw their work published only after Soviet imperial ambitions in ideology died a hard death, only to be revived far too soon amid the expanses of what at least some of them would inevitably see as an eager-to-expand Wasteland.

The work of these poets wasn't minimalist in the sense that they had little to say; quite the contrary, it captured the frustration, suppressed ambitions and hidden energy of several generations of Russian people. As Vassily Kandinsky once put it, 'Even absolute silence is a loud speech.' Joseph Brodsky in one of his lectures compared Mark Strand and Charles Simic, well-established American 'poets of silence', as he called them, to 'unofficial' Russian poets who had to dwell in silence, due to having no other literary space. The Leningrad poet Kari Unksova wrote about 'the bitterness of seclusion', whereas Rea Nikonova, a poet from the South of Russia, even produced a catalogue of different kinds of silence. She knew very well what she was talking about, as she first lived in Yeysk, a small Russian town on coast of the Azov Sea – and then on the other shores of exile, in Germany, until her untimely death.

'After Pasternak, Russian poetry sustained a pause,' the late Genrikh Sapgir used to say. It was destined to be a long pause. In fact, the generation of Russian writers that emerged in the early 60s grew up reading and studying in college Russian poetry from the 1920s. Some of them were particularly inspired by Boris Pasternak and Osip Mandelstam, others by Velimir Khlebnikov and other Russian Futurist poets. What appeared in Soviet 'fat magazines' in those times were, to quote Anna Akhmatova, 'rhymed editorials', or otherwise third-rate imitations of Symbolist poetry from the late nineteenth century. In the 1960s and 1970s, Yevgeny Kropivnitsky, Genrikh Sapgir, Vsevolod Nekrasov and Igor Kholin were the most prominent among the Moscow writers that came to be associated with the now well-known Lianozovo group named after the town on the outskirts of Moscow where the informal leader of the group, Yevgeny Kropivnitsky, lived. This name was given to the group by the KGB, but the group members came to like it and adopted it.

These poets sought out new models and positions, and exploited the possibilities of inserting common speech directly into their texts. Each of them had a Dostoyevskian eye for everyday Russian life, which made their work immediately accessible. No wonder that they at once found themselves uncomfortable with authority and orthodoxy, and also with the authorities and the Orthodox Church, suppressed under the Communists but still powerful, as far as the minds of the Russians were concerned. These were real rebels, unlike a few other Russian poets who enjoyed virtual pop-star status, unthinkable if transposed to other parts of Europe. In reality, the latter were far from any sort of protest against Soviet totalitarianism and therefore could not be regarded as anything else but naughty children of the regime.

The idea of a cultural centre was particularly dispiriting for those who were geographically based far from Moscow and therefore felt marginalised. Gennady Aigi is typical of the rise of poets who settled down in the Russian capital and preferred to write in Russian rather than in their mother tongues, in this case Chuvash; no wonder that his poems sounded so fresh and enriched the Russian language to such a great extent. Poems by Gennady Aigi are derived entirely from individual words and sometimes from single syllables and sounds. He created his own language, an independent and unique speech or, if you prefer, chant. Interestingly, Gennady Aigi made a great deal of translations and so participated in an exchange of 'poetic air' with other cultures.

Russia has always been a huge and bipolar country. The difference between Moscow and Leningrad/St. Petersburg poetry can make one feel that these two cities are located in different countries. The so-called New Leningrad School of Poetry that emerged in Leningrad at the beginning of the 1970s was extremely influential in the then seemingly invisible culture of the Russian literary underground. The group included the Nobel Prize winner Joseph Brodsky, as well as Sergey Stratanovsky, Viktor Krivulin, and Elena Shvarts. Viktor Krivulin's obsession with Dante set him on a mental journey through the circles of some sort of hell, or 'counterfeit Eden', which he found in his urban habitation, but also inside the minds of many of his countrymen. Sergey Stratanovsky, now perceived by many as the leading living St. Petersburg poet, displays determination to remind us of the great cultural traditions of St. Petersburg, the former capital of Russia, and their deterioration under the Communists.

Of course, it was no surprise that magic realism became one of the main trends in Russian poetry. The great figures of Nikolai Gogol and Mikhail Bulgakov cast long shadows over Russian writing. In his essay, *Catastrophes in the Air*, Joseph Brodsky defined the way in which writers of that strain worked. He described the metamorphosis of Andrei Platonov, the prominent Russian magic realist of the early twentieth century, novelist and short story writer, in the following terms: 'He tells the story about his own language, which turns out to be capable of generating a fictitious world, and then falls into dependence on it.' The language used by most of the Russian magic realists, e.g. by Viktor Krivulin and Sergey Stratanovsky, has always been saturated with metaphors. The first major Russian magic realist poet, Mandelstam, was as much of a revolutionary as any Bolshevik, and Russian poetry could never be the same after his verse was published.

Incidentally, many St. Petersburg poets of the 1990s seemed to take after Mandelstam and Brodsky who had been exiled in 1972; others developed pretty sophisticated poetry according to the good old canons. Kari Unksova and Gennady Alexeyev were one of the first St. Petersburg poets ever to choose *vers libre* as their poetic device. Their texts are quite recognisable as having their roots in their emotional expressionism. They preserved a relatively unadulterated singleness in the first person, as did Vladimir Earle in his rather unusual melodious poems written in the 1970s.

The work collected here documents poetry in Russia responding to the challenges of the dark years of Russian history. These poets deserve to be remembered, especially now that Russia has more political prisoners than were held in the Soviet Union during the final five years of its existence.

Anatoly Kudryavitsky
Dublin, Ireland

Геннадий Айги

Путь

Когда нас никто не любит
начинаем
любить матерей

Когда нам никто не пишет
вспоминаем
старых друзей

И слова произносим уже лишь потому
что молчанье нам страшно
а движенья опасны

В конце же – в случайных запущенных парках
плачем от жалких труб
жалких оркестров

Gennady Aigi

Our Way

When nobody likes us
we learn
how to love our mothers

When nobody writes to us
we call to mind
old friends

And we utter a few words – simply because
we're scared of silence
and deem any movement dangerous

And in the end we sob in a park overgrown
with shrubs as we hear the pitiable trumpets
of a pitiable brass band

Клен на окраине города

какое же во дереве
безмолвие
как будто в целом мире
есть только он один – сентябрьско-тихий клен!
о нет о больше... – словно то присутствие:
ты – перед дверью некой
притих и знаешь: есть – теперь лишь это «там»
что более понятий
без объяснения... – вхожденье же возможно
(уход – покой – забвенье)
ценою лишь одной: не видеть более
вот этот клен – сентябрьский

A Maple on the Outskirts of Town

how much silence is hidden
inside the tree
as if nothing else exists in the wide world but
this quiet September maple!
o no there is much more to it – like some kind of
presence: you stand before some door
you're calm and knowing: the only important thing
is in there – and it's bigger than any concept
no need for explanation but entry is possible
(departure – peace – oblivion)
at the cost of not seeing anymore
this quiet September maple

Из цикла «Тишина»

а те с того самого времени как начали
видеть свет божий
стали впервые теперь различать
черное от белого
и пришли в восторг и торопятся уже сообщить
вот это – белое
а это черное

Silence

...and some people have been trying
to tell the black from the white
since the very first moment
they saw the daylight...
they succeed at long last
and go into raptures and hasten
to bring to our notice: this is white
and that is black

Дождь

и моросит и утихает
как будто возится сама с собой 'случайность'

(как 'одаренность' годная
лишь для набросков жалких)

как будто 'есть' 'живет'

(в кругу – как я – ненужности)

The Rain

drizzles and subsides
as if 'fortuity' is romping with itself

(just as a 'talent'
capable only of middling sketches)

as if 'it exists' really exists

(in the circle of uselessness –
exactly where I find myself)

Метель в окне

В.Я.

Метель в окне и стены комнаты
и затеряв меня давно во вьюге дом
рисунков на стенах собрание как в прятках
как в юности – в ее далекой свежести
когда (метель) окно: как тайну: ладила
свое: то там то здесь:
немного поправляя

Snowstorm in My Window

for V.Y.

a snowstorm in my window – and my room's
walls – my house has long lost sight of me in a blizzard
the collection of drawings on the walls
playing hide-and-seek with me – the way it used to be
in my youth in bygone days of freshness when it (the snowstorm)
decorated my window building a mystery
adjusting every little thing:
now here, now there

Юрий Айхенвальд

Смерть Художника

Посвящается художнику Л.,
с которым я был в одной камере
и который, как я слышал,
умер в тюремной больнице.

Вот так резинкою стирают
Рисунок конченный с бумаги.
Лежит художник, умирает.
Не хочет супа из салаки.
Лежит, пришпиленный к пространству.
Его стирают.
Делать нечего!..
Глядит тюремное начальство,
Как белизна в окне просвечивает.
А он толкует о Моне,
Рисует спичками горелыми
На оборотной стороне
Коробок из-под сигарет.
То черный цвет, то серый цвет
Опять перекрывает белое...

Yuri Aikenvald

An Artist's Death

In memory of the artist L.,
with whom I shared a prison cell,
and who, as I was told,
died in a prison hospital.

This is how they use a rubber to erase
A perfect drawing from a sheet of paper.
The artist is dying.
He doesn't want a herring soup.
He's lying there pinned to infinite space.
He gets erased –
And nothing can be done.
The prison bosses stare at the whiteness
In the window that shines through.
Meantime, the artist talks about Monet
And draws something with burnt matches
On the back of a
Cigarette box.
A black stroke, then a grey one.
The whiteness, again, is overlapping...

* * *

Памяти Варлама Шаламова

Черный снег на фоне белом.
Белом,
словно омертвелом, –
вот колымская судьба.
Вот такое
поле боя
алкашу – для водопоя,
а Шемяке – для суда.
Лица черные.
Землею
обожженные.
Золою
ставшие.
Экклезиаст
говорил про вещи эти:
– Почернеет все на свете.
Волк не выдаст –
Вошь продаст.
Не хотите – не ходите.
Голубым богам кадите.
Ждите
милостей в ответ,
Что в основе негатива?
Люди жили?
Эко диво!
Век в колымских перспективах
пишет свой автопортрет.

In Memory of Varlam Shalamov

Black snow against a white background...
White is similar
to dead –
this is Kolyma's fate for you.
This is a battlefield:
for a drunkard, the challenge
of water drinking,
for a kangaroo, the court challenge.
Faces are black.
Burnt
by the soil.
Turned
into ashes.
Ecclesiastes
mentioned such things:
Everything in the world will go black.
God willing, a wolf will help you,
and a louse will sell you out.
If you don't want to go, don't go.
Burn incense for the blue gods.
Wait
for benefits in return.
Why so negative?
So some people survived?
What a marvel!
The century at Kolyma's vista
paints its self-portrait.

Гамлет в 1937 году

А вы слышали песни
Соловьев в Соловках?
– Ну-ка, выстройся, плесень,
С кайлами в руках!
Ты, очкастый, чего невнимателен?
Исключаешься ты
Из рабочей семьи,
И катись ты с земли
К Божьей Матери!

И распались кружки,
Раздружились дружки,
Потому что история
Любит прыжки,
Потому что безумный
Плясун на канате
Ненавидит
Времен пресловутую связь.
– Датский принц!
Вашу шляпу и шпагу!
Копайте!
Ибо Дания ваша
Без боя сдалась.

И распались кружки,
Раздобрели дружки,
Потому что история
Любит прыжки.
– По грошу
Положите в церковные кружки!
Помолитесь
За целые ваши горшки
Божьей Матери-Деве,
Пречистой старушке!

Hamlet in 1937

Ever heard a nightingale
Singing solo in the Solovki Camp?
Come on, line up, you mould
With pickaxes!
You, the four-eyed one, pay attention.
We'll kick you out of
Our proletariat family,
So you can roll off this planet
To the Mother of God!

And the circles fell apart,
Friendships fell apart,
Because history
Likes leaping;
Because the mad
Rope dancer
Hates
The time that's 'out of joints.'
You, the Danish prince!
Give us your hat and your sword!
Start digging!
For your Denmark
Surrendered without a fight.

And the circles fell apart,
Friends on the outside got fat,
Because history
Likes leaping.
Put your pennies
In church collection baskets!
Say your prayers
To the Virgin Mary,
The holy old woman,
So your pots remain intact.

Датским принцем
Нельзя называться без Дании.
Вот земля и лопата –
Ваше «быть иль не быть».
Датский принц,
Что нелепей, смешнее, бездарнее,
Чем о званье, призванье своем
Не забыть!?

Датский принц
Удаляется в смутные дебри.
Он лежит,
Умирает на призрачной койке,
Он молчит,
С королевским достоинством терпит
И, конечно, заплатит
За все неустойки...

А в квартире
Кончалось счастливое детство:
Образованный мальчик,
Из хорошей семьи.
И за что-то ему
Перешло, как наследство,
Званье Датского Принца,
Короля
Без земли.

You can't be called a Danish prince
If there's no Denmark.
Here's the soil and the shovel,
Your 'to be or not to be.'
A Danish prince...
What can be funnier, more ridiculous,
More dull than remembering your standing,
Your talent where you are now?

The Danish prince
Retreats to some hazy wilderness.
He is lying on a ghostly bed,
Dying;
He's silent,
He endures all things with royal dignity,
And, of course, he'll pay
The penalty...

And in some apartment,
There's a well-educated boy
From a good family.
His happy childhood ends;
The title of Danish Prince
Passes to him
As an inheritance,
So he will now be a landless
King.

Юлий Даниэль

На Библейские Темы

Да будет ведомо всем,
Кто
Я
Есть:
Рост – 177;
Вес – 66;
Руки мои тонки,
Мышцы мои слабы,
И презирают станки
Кривую моей судьбы;
От роду – сорок лет,
Прожитых напролет,
Время настало – бред
Одолеваю вброд:
Против МЕНЯ – войска
Против МЕНЯ – штыки
Против МЕНЯ – тоска
(Руки мои тонки);
Против МЕНЯ – в зенит
Брошен радиоклич.
Серого зданья гранит
Входит со мною в клинч;
Можно меня смолоть
И с потрохами съесть
Хрупкую эту плоть
(Вес – 66),
Можно меня согнуть
(От роду – 40 лет),
Можно обрушить муть

Yuri Daniel

On Biblical Themes

To whom it may concern,
My
Details,
Measurements:
I am 5 feet 9 inches tall,
I weigh 145.5 pounds;
My arms are thin,
My muscles weak;
Machines despise
The curve of my fate;
I am forty years old,
Each year lived thoroughly through;
Now the time has come – I cross
The stream of nonsense at a ford;
Against me, the troops;
Against me, the bayonets;
Against me, my yearning
(My arms are thin);
Against me, radio announcements
Thrust into the air.
The grey granite building
Clinches with me;
They can grind me
And eat me alive,
My flesh is fragile
(I weigh 145.5 pounds),
They can bend me
(I'm forty),
They can drown me in the swamp

Митингов и газет;
Можно меня стереть –
Двинуть махиной всей,
Жизни отрезать треть
(Рост – 177).
– Ясен исход борьбы!..
– Время себя жалеть!..
(Мышцы мои слабы)
Можно обрушить плеть,
Можно затмить мне свет,
Остановить разбег!..
Можно и можно...
Нет.
Я ведь – не человек:
(Рост – 177)
Я твой окоп, Добро,
(Вес – 66)
Я – смотровая щель,
(Руки мои тонки)
Пушки твоей ядро,
(Мышцы мои слабы)
Камень в твоей праще.

Of hostile gatherings and newspapers;
They can erase me,
Put forward the mighty Colossus against me,
Cut off a third of my life
(I am 5 feet 9 inches tall).
I see the clear outcome of this fight.
It's time to feel sorry for myself
(My muscles are weak).
Their whip can crash down my back,
They can extinguish my light,
Stop my life run.
They can do many things to me...
But no.
I'm not a person
(I am 5 feet 9 inches tall),
I'm your trench, the world's Goodness
(I weigh 145.5 pounds),
I am the viewing chink
(My arms are thin);
I am a cannonball in your bombard
(My muscles are weak),
A stone in your sling.

Дом

В окно я глянул и увидел дом.
Обычный дом – немыслимое чудо:
Он был семи – или восьмиэтажный,
И в первом этаже был магазин,
А выше были окна без решеток,
И каждое окно освещено
Своим особым светом, непохожим
На свет соседних. Это оттого,
Что там на окнах были занавески
И были шторы – словом, было то,
Чем люди отгораживаться вправе
От посторонних взглядов. Я, однако,
Сумел глазами памяти увидеть,
Узнать лицо потерянного рая:
Там были стулья и цветы на окнах,
Когда-то презиравшиеся мною
Цветы в горшках, зеленые божки,
С которых пыль стирают по субботам;
Там лампы в потолки не уходили,
Не прятались за мутным плексигласом,
А рдели в кринолинах абажуров,
Собой венчали шаткие торшеры,
Со стен свисали... Там на книжных полках
Лежали неожиданные вещи:
Шнурки от туфель, биллиардный шарик,
Чулок с иголкой в штопке, позабытый
Из-за гостей, нагрянувших врасплох;
Еще рецепт – его уже с неделю
Никто никак не может отыскать ...
Там были скатерти, на них ножи и вилки –
Орава режущих и колющих предметов...
Там, в этом доме, было много женщин –
Не медсестер и не стенографисток,
А просто женщин. В платьицах домашних

A House

I looked out the window, and saw a house,
A seven- or eight-storey building;
An ordinary one, but also quite incredible.
There was a shop on the ground level;
The windows on the other floors had no bars,
And each was lit up with some special
Variety of light, and there were
No identical ones. This was because
The windows had curtains
And blinds, the things that people use,
And rightfully so, to fence off
Strangers' gazes. However, I managed
To see, with my memory's eyes, the face
Of the lost paradise, and it looked familiar:
There were chairs, flowers on the windowsills,
And house-plants in pots, the green idols,
To be dusted on Saturdays;
O, how I used to despise them!
The electric bulbs weren't embedded in the ceilings
Or concealed by mat plastic;
They hung inside the frock-shaped *abat-jours*,
Or crowned the wobbly standard lamps,
Or hung down from the walls... The book-shelves
harboured bric-a-brac, like
Shoe-laces, or a snooker ball,
A stocking with a protruding needle left behind
Since the surprise arrival of some guests,
And also a mislaid prescription sought for
For the whole duration of the week.
There were tablecloths laid out with knives and forks,
Abundant sharp and pointed cutlery...
Women were abundant too;
Not nurses or stenographers,
Just women, wearing casual dresses,

Они, сколовши волосы небрежно
И рукава по локоть засучив,
Купали в новых ванночках младенцев,
Со лба к затылку отгоняя воду,
Чтоб мыльной пене в глазки не попасть;
И отблеск розовых мелькающих локтей
Ложился сполохом на сердце, обещая
Округлое и теплое свершенье
Потом, когда погаснет в доме свет ...
Да, я забыл сказать, что по фасаду
На доме было множество балконов,
Где стыли на ветру велосипеды
И в сети гамаков шли косяками
Проворные снежинки...
                              Дом трещал –
Его неудержимо распирало,
Давило изнутри избытком жизни!
В нем жило все – от шпильки головной,
От кошки и собаки до нескладных
Подростков с неуклюжими руками,
Украдкой сочиняющих стихи.
И алые частицы этой жизни
Сквозь кладку стен, как запах, проходили,
Летели сквозь зашторенные окна
Ко мне, ко мне, к откинутой фрамуге
Окна, перед которым я стоял,
На стол взобравшись. Целых полминуты
Я прикасался к человечьей жизни.
Потом я спрыгнул на пол. Вот и всё.
... Я знаю, что неловки эти строки,
Что мой товарищ глянет неподкупно,
Серьезно покачает головой
И скажет мне: «А что как это проза,
Да и плохая?» – «Да, скажу я, – да!
Плохая проза. Хуже не бывает...»

With their hair jauntily pinned back
And sleeves rolled up to their elbows;
They bathed their babies in spanking-new baby-baths
Driving the water from their foreheads to their crowns
To keep their tiny eyes soap-free,
And a sparkle of pink flickering elbows resembled
A ray of light illuminating the heart, promising
Some round-shaped warm accomplishment at a
Later hour, when the lights would go out across the house...
Ah, I forgot to mention that there were
Many balconies on the front façade,
Where bicycles rested, frozen in the wind,
And flocks of agile snowflakes hurried
Into the nets of hammocks...
                              The house was
Crackling, bursting, pressured from inside
By an excess of life!
All things in it were alive – from hair-slides
To cats and dogs to awkward
Teenagers who scribble poetry
With their clumsy hands.
And the scarlet particles of this life were percolating
Through the masonry walls, like a smell;
They flew through the panes and curtains
To me, to me, as, having climbed the table,
I was standing in front of an open
Casement window. For half a minute
I partook a human life. Then I
Jumped down to the floor. And that was it.
... I know these lines are clumsy,
And my friend will cast a steady glance at me
And shake his earnest head, and
Say to me: 'What if all this is prose – and not the best
Variety of it?' 'Oh, yes,' I will reply, 'Oh, sure thing!
Just bad prose. Worse than any...'

Из поэмы «А в это время...»

Тому уже три века,
Тому всего три дня,
Как Муза дальних странствий
Взревела под окном.
По кочкам и по строчкам
Поволокла меня
В неукротимом газике,
Бывалом «вороном».
Дорога, о, дорога!
Жестокая жара...
Дорога, о, дорога!
Железные морозы.
Ведут машину нашу
Слепые шофера,
Раздавливая скатами
Наивные вопросы.
Ни очага, ни света,
Ни птиц, ни тишины,
А только километры
Качающихся суток,
И наши судьбы пестрые
Силком сопряжены
В бегущих по дорогам
Решетчатых сосудах.
К далекой остановке
Протянута ладонь ...
Подъемы и уклоны,
То кувырком, то юзом ...
А что же было раньше,
А что же было ДО
Со всеми нами – этим
Подведомственным грузом?

From 'In the Meantime...'

Three days ago,
Three centuries ago
The Muse of Distant Wanderings
Yelled under my window.
She dragged me away
Past all the tussocks and the printed lines
In an indomitable jeep,
A Black Maria.
Oh, road, this road!
How fierce the heat...
Oh, road, this road!
The iron frost.
Blind drivers
At the rudder,
Crushing naive questions
Under wheels.
No hearth, no light,
No birds, no silence,
Only kilometres
From all these swinging days,
And our motley fates are
Conjugated in a forceful manner
In trellised vessels
All along the road.
Palms are outstretched
Towards a distant stop...
Uphill and downhill,
First skidding and then somersaulting...
So what has occurred before?
What has happened prior to THIS
With all of us, the State-dependent
Cargo?

Владимир Эрль

* * *

Я в осень вошел, как во взгляд,
как в тихий туман реки.
Зеленые тростники
качались зачем-то вдали...
Я в осень вошел, как в реку,
охваченную тишью снов.
И легионы слов
качались где-то вдали.
Я в осень вошел, как в слова,
потерянные кем-то вдали.

Vladimir Earle

Autumn

I entered into autumn as into a glance,
or into a quiet mist on the river's face.
Green canes
were swaying in the distance.
I entered into autumn as into the river
embraced by the silence of dreams.
Myriads of words
were swaying in the distance.
I entered into autumn as into the words
somebody had lost in the distance.

* * *

Преграда сна –
как ветер, рвущий в клочья
деревья гибкие.
Вчера – я снова жил.
Сегодня – только сплю;
проходит вереница
пустых мечтаний.
Волны ль это –
или песок – сыпучий, легкий и бесцветный?
Как будто дождь...

The Barrier of Sleep

The barrier of sleep –
is like the wind that rips these supple trees
to pieces.
Yesterday I lived again.
Today I'm only sleeping.
A row of empty dreams
passes before my eyes.
Are these the waves? Or maybe
sand, free-flowing, colourless and light?
It resembles rain...

* * *

Когда люди имеют мнения,
они обмениваются ими.
Когда люди не имеют мнений,
они обмениваются отсутствием мнений.

Opinions

When people have opinions,
they swap them.
When people have no opinions,
they swap the absence of opinions.

Эвридика

Пламя свечи виновато марьяжит.
Меняется форма, рождается шорох –
Орфея плач. Он слышит
удар руки по струнам звонкой лиры...
Связует нить воззрения паука,
повисшего над миром
мельчайших тканей, –
тянется за словом моим паутина –
златого дня немыслимый конец.

И пьет Орфей настой из терпких слов,
забывшись сном, над лирою склоняясь
и наблюдая гладь
сиреневого Стикса.

Eurydice

A candle flickers guiltily.
The flame changes its shape, and causes a rustle,
which is the weeping of Orpheus. He hears
his hand strike the strings of the resonant lyre...
The thread of spider's thoughts
the one that hangs above the world
of fine-grained substance
cobweb trails my words,
such an unthinkable end of the golden day.

And so Orpheus drinks an extract of bitter words,
which leaves him sunk into a reverie,
bent over the lyre and the glassy surface
of the lilac Styx.

* * *

О!
О, чешуя на руках!
ребра мои окружает вода
плещет плавник за спиной
воздух сгущается.

О!
О, тени в подводных садах –
иногда
вырастают стеной
позади.

Under Water

Ah!
O these scales on my hands!
my ribs are surrounded by water
the fin behind my back makes splashes
the air thickens.

Ah!
O these shadows in the underwater gardens –
sometimes they
build themselves up like a wall
behind you.

Юрий Галансков

* * *

Ночь темна.
Луна.
Она, конечно, не одна.
И я совсем не одинок,
вот-вот – и прозвенит звонок.
Услышу в дверь условный стук,
вскочу, схвачу пожатье рук,
надену плащ,
и мы уйдем
почти
под проливным дождем.
Уйдем,
и надо полагать –
идем кого-то низвергать.

Yuri Galanskov

Night

Dark is the night.
The moon.
Not lonesome, of course.
And I'm not truly alone:
the bell will ring any moment now.
I'll hear a secret knock on the door,
get up, get a grab handshake,
put on a raincoat –
and we'll come out
into the teaming rain.
We'll leave
and, purportedly,
we'll go
to get somebody overthrown.

Из поэмы «Подснежник»

Искренне,
чисто,
наивно
и грубо
грудь отдаю для душевно нищих.
Вижу –
ваши иссохшие губы
ищут.

From 'Snowdrop'

Sincerely,
purely,
naively,
and unmannerly
I give my bosom to the poor in spirit.
I can see
your withered lips
yearning.

Конструкция

«Папа, снимите хомутики», –
маленький мальчик изрёк.
«Видишь, сыночек, прутики;
а если ещё поперёк?..

Дай-ка тетрадку в клетку.
Здесь нарисуй
глаза,
птичку,
солнце
и ветку,
и на щеке – слеза...»

И на тетрадке в клетку
тихо рисует зверёк
птичку,
солнце
и ветку
в прутиках поперёк...

Design

Dad, remove the blinkers,
a little boy uttered.
Do you see the twigs, son;
what if you draw across?

Let's take a squared notebook.
Draw in it
the eyes,
a bird,
the Sun,
and a branch,
and a tear on the cheek...

And the little beast
draws quietly in the squared notebook –
first a bird,
then the Sun
and a branch
behind bars...

Из «Человеческого манифеста»

Министрам, вождям и газетам –
не верьте!

Вставайте, лежащие ниц!
Видите, шарики атомной смерти
у Мира в могилах глазниц.
Вставайте!
Вставайте!
Вставайте!
О, алая кровь бунтарства!
Идите и доломайте
гнилую тюрьму государства!
Идите по трупам пугливых
тащить для голодных людей
чёрные бомбы, как сливы,
на блюдища площадей.

From *The Human Manifesto*

Ministers, leaders, newspapers –
believe none of them!

Get up, the prostrated!
Can't you see the balls of atomic death
inside the World's grave sockets?
Get up!
Get up!
Get up!
O the red blood of rebellion!
Go and smash
the rotten prison state!
Walk over the corpses of the shy,
drag black plum-like bombs
onto the dishes of the squares
for all the hungry.

Утро

Горящим лезвием зарницы
восток поджег крыло вороны.
И весело запели птицы
в сетях немой и черной кроны.
Запутал ноги пешеходу
туман, нависший над травой...
И кто-то лез беззвучно в воду
огромной рыжей головой.

Morning

With the burning blade of lightning
the East set fire to a crow's wing.
And the birds began to sing merrily
in the cobwebs of a tree's dumb dark crown.
A walker tripped over the fog hanging
just above the grass...
And somebody, in silence, threw himself
into the water head first. His huge red head...

Наталья Горбаневская

* * *

Кто бросает веревку
в вечную бездну колодца,
где укололась о веретенце
осиротелая птаха?
Камень пробьет воронку
и вызовет долгие кольца,
и отразится солнце,
холодное, словно плаха.

Штихелем вырыто
в медной доске,
отпечатано
в сто листов
все, что выла ты,
лежа в песке,
вся печаль твоя,
весь твой стон –

и тихая пауза
между двумя
молчаниями...
И лодка парусная
глядит на меня,
отчаливая.

Natalia Gorbanevskaya

Printed

Who throws a rope
into the eternal chasm of the well,
where a spindle pricks
an orphaned bird?
The stone will fall through the funnel
creating rings on the water,
and the Sun's reflection will be
cold as a chopping block.

All that you howled
while lying on the sand,
your sorrow,
your moans
get engraved
on a copper board,
and then
one hundred sheets
get printed,

and also the quietude,
the pause between two
silences...
And a sailing boat
gazes at me
as it floats away.

* * *

Ничего и не сыщется проще
процарапать хвостатый щекочущий росчерк,
ничего и милее,
чем уметь свое имя, его не имея,
по слогам, по растянутым гласным
интонировать горлом безгласным
в клочковатом пространстве
анонимных страстей и троллейбусной тряски,
перепойного транса и транспортных петель,
в третий раз в этом горле удушенный петел
на заре не кричит и зарю не вещует
и, не чуя себя от бессонницы, щурит
слепотою куриной припухшие веки...
И в разлуке навеки голос в клетке, пичуга на ветке.

Name

Nothing is easier than
scratching your tailed tickling signature;
nothing is nicer
than, knowing your name without having one,
to intone it with your mute throat
syllable by syllable, stretching the vowels,
in the ragged space
of anonymous passions, on shaking buses,
amid an intoxication, in a transport loop.
A half-strangled rooster doesn't cry out
Inside this throat for the third time, at dawn,
doesn't announce a new day's arrival, and, anxious
because of insomnia, squints his blind swollen eyelids...
In eternal separation, a voice in a cage
          and a wren on a branch.

* * *

И не до красоты, не до расчета
златых сечений в переполохе сечи,
и речи глохнут. Одних щитов защита
бряцает о мечи, упряча плечи
от злых сечцов. Сочти своих осталых
на опустевшем поле. На вокзалах
гудки взвиваются к стеклянным сводам,
уста усмешкой сведены донельзя,
до эха замирающего рельса
далече. Ежели дар речи отдан
битв отголоскам, вагонов перестуку
на стыках, гулу клокочущего пульса
из-под запястья. Одолевая скуку,
язык зашевелился, и запнулся,
и вновь в захлопнутой улегся пасти
доотоспаться. Не было б напасти
похуже этакой. Летящих стай
дай клич и клекот, вслед за взлетом птичьим
своди мне челюсти косноязычьем
льдяным, как стылая по сече сталь.

Speech

No time for beauty, or for calculating
the golden ratio in a battle's commotion,
and so the speech dies down. The shield
clanks against the swords, protecting the shoulders
from the warriors of evil. Count your survivours
on the deserted field. At the railway stations,
the sounds of hooters soar to the glass ceilings;
the mouths splay in crooked grins
to the echo of vibrating rails that comes
from far away. What if the gift of speech
is spent on battle echoes, on carriages that rattle
at the joints, or on the humming of the pulse that
bubbles in your wrist? Overcoming boredom,
your tongue stirs and falters,
and then again lies down inside the shut mouth
to get some sleep. An adversity can't be
any worse than that. Give me the cry and the screech
of the flying flocks, and, when the birds take off,
make my jaws freeze, leave me tongue-tied
and ice-cold like the steel used in a deadly combat.

* * *

Блажен эпический поэт,
кому дыхания хватает,
не перехватывает горло
вполслова...

Poet

Blessed is the epic poet
with a higher amplitude of breath,
with no lump in his throat
mid-sentence...

* * *

Телеграфный переулок.
Черная 'Волга'
гонится за мной,
въезжает на тротуар.
Сон 69-го года.

Lane, Moscow

Telegraph Lane.
A black Volga
chases me,
mounts the pavement.
A dream from 1969.

Игорь Холин

Плач

Удивительная способность
Человека
Плакать
Вызывать жалость
Таким странным образом
Почему
Не плачут
Звери
Дома
Автомашины
Мне могут заметить
Что они тоже
Плачут
И что не всегда
Проливают слезы
От избытка чувств
Иногда просто
Соринка
Попала в глаз
Или что-то
Но я не об этом
Я о всемирном плаче
Когда содрогается
Вселенная
Когда все сливается
В единый
Вскрик
Вздох

Igor Kholin

Weeping

Isn't it amazing,
This human ability
To cry
And appeal for pity
In such a strange way?
Why animals
Don't cry,
And houses
And cars?
Somebody may say
That they cry, too,
But seldom
Shed tears
Out of the fullness
Of the heart.
Sometimes
A speck of dust
Or something
Gets into somebody's eye
But this is not
What I'm talking about.
I want to tell you
About world-wide weeping
When the universe
Shudders
And everything merges into
A single scream,
A deep-drawn sigh.

* * *

Камера
Инженера Крамера
В ней
Идет обработка людей
В смысле
Единства идей
Тук
Тук
Тук
Работает ультразвук
У Нилина
Лишняя извилина
Жилину
Добавить извилину

Cramer's Camera

Engineer Cramer
Invented a camera
Inside it
They are processing people
To achieve
Unification of ideas
Rat-tat
Rat-tat
Rat-tat
Ultrasound in action
Nilin has
An extra gyrus
Zhilin
To be added a gyrus

Из военного цикла

Командир батареи
Безусый
Парнишка
Рассматривал в бинокль
Поле
Утыканное
Ромашками
И васильками
Затем
Вдохнул
Полной грудью
Окопную вонь
Крикнул
Огооонь
И все полетело
Вверх тормашками

From the War River

The gun-commander
A young lad
Wearing no
Moustache
Used his field glass
To examine
The field
All about were
Dotted daisies
And cornflowers
The lad breathed in
The trench stink
And screamed:
Fire!
Topsy-turvyness
The world is in a mess

* * *

Ни звезды
Ни креста
Ни черта
Волосы
Вместо травы
Торчат
Из земли
На братской могиле

Common Grave

No stars
No crosses
No nothing
Instead of grass
Hair
Sticks
Out of the ground
At the common grave

* * *

Одни говорят
Что я гений
Я говорю
Это
Действительно так
Другие говорят
Бездарен
Я подтверждаю
Третьи говорят
Я убил человека
Киваю головой
Все что говорят люди
Правда
Сотканная
Из пустоты

Truths

Some say
I am a man of genius
I never
Deny it
Others assert that
I am dull
I readily
Agree
Somebody alleges that
I murdered a man
I nod
Everything people say
Is a truth
Woven from
Emptiness

Виктор Кривулин

Рысь

золотоглазую мы не заметили Рысь
когда она следит не щурясь, не мигая
за солнцем, нет, за митингом:
сошлись
они стоят как тишина большая
защитники всего что ползает плывет
что ходит посуху и над землей летает...
но поздно уже... вечер... холодает
и, постояв, расходится народ

Victor Krivulin

Lynx

that golden-eyed Lynx, we didn't notice it
as it watched the Sun,
oh no, it watched the meeting,
not even blinking...
they gather and stand still like greater silence,
those protectors of everything that crawls, or swims,
or walks on dry land, or flies over...
but it is getting late... and growing cold...
and soon the people drift apart

Пока мы изобретали рай

когда мы конструировали Запад
на сорока внутрисоветских языках
как некий Рай в золовых рукавах
как Ханаан, какой не занят
никем – и только нам обетован, –
мы видели египетские казни
вокруг себя, но жили безопасней
Обломова: схожденье на диван
святого духа с эмигрантским чтивом
портрет Набокова с пурпурною каймой...

когда ходил Господь по нищенским квартирам
и призывал на родину, домой –
в Европу, в Индию ли, в Палестину,
где Пуп Земли, а мы всегда не там...

While We Invented Paradise

while we constructed the West
in the forty Soviet languages,
just like some sort of paradise in our ashen hands,
or like Canaan, unoccupied and promised
to ourselves – we saw the punishment of Egypt
but lived much safer than Oblomov:
we would come down, the way the Holy Spirit did,
to a sofa, holding an émigré journal
and facing a portrait of Nabokov in the purple frame...

meanwhile, the Lord called on our beggarly abodes
and summoned us to our real homelands,
to Europe, or to India, sometimes to Palestine,
the hub of the Universe
where we are always missing...

Книги и люди

худо, конечно, с какого конца ни возьми
но может быть, из-за того
полуослепшие книги тоже казались людьми
и скрывали преступное с ними родство

прятали а если за стенкой затихал сосед –
бережно – как шуршит папиросный слой! –
обнажали какой-нибудь порфироносный портрет
полоску с гольбеиновой Пьетой

Books and Men

indeed, it was bad from any point of view
but maybe because of that
weak-sighted books acquired a strange resemblance
to people and so had to conceal forbidden kinship

however, when a neighbour calmed down behind the wall
they would uncover cautiously –
the flimsy paper rustling timidly –
some regal portrait – or Holbein's Pietà

Над гранитной фабрикой

над гранитной фабричкой агатовая пыль
крошка ониксовая опаловая труха

тут тебе и творчество и лаборатория стиха
и традиции и национальный стиль
полудрагоценный камень превращается в утиль
в пепельницу или в тельце петуха

и полуслепой приемщицы ОТК
слабый штемпель
не смываемый
на века

Over the Granite Factory

in the air over the small granite factory, there are
hyalite crumbs, tiny bits of onyx and agathic dust

a classic example of a creative workshop
and poetic laboratory, a real booster of traditions
and the national style... semiprecious stone turns
into rubbish, like a figurine of a rooster or an ash-tray –

and a quality inspector, the weak-sighted female,
stamps each object in the same way
with a pale mark,
never to be erased

Милые ошибки властей

эти милые сердцу ошибки властей
эти слабые волосы еле прикрывшие темя
розоватое!
это паренье частей
расчлененного Тела... и Небо стоит надо всеми
с выраженьем усталости, как бы заранье простив
что движения наши подобны растеньям
что назойлив простой эфемерный мотив
поражающий не превращеньем
но повторами
словно древнейший орнамент
искажает лицо:
это волчье, а то поросячье,
в лучшем случае – птичье...
подложный Эдем
перед нами разложен и властвует нами
и в глаза не глядит – но глаза по-животному прячет,
зарывая куда-то их, где хорошо и незряче:

где возможно прожить не увидясь ни с кем

Sweet Mistakes of the Authorities

o those sweet mistakes of the authorities,
this thin hair hardly covering the pink
top of the head!
this soaring flight of the parts
of a dismembered Body...
the Sky hangs over us, showing signs of fatigue,
as if it has already excused us for the vegetative way
we move and for that annoyingly simple, ephemeral motive,
subject to an amazing number of repetitions
but never to development –
just as an ancient ornament
distorts a face:
this one is wolfish, and that one pig-like,
or bird-like, at best...
counterfeit Eden
is displayed before us... it owns us
and never looks at us – but, like an animal,
aims its glance at some cosy blind spot

where one can live not seeing anyone at all

Евгений Кропивницкий

Из Книги '100 Советов Самому Себе'

Будь смиренен и не злись.
Всегда кайся, ибо ты грешен, как и все.
Старайся все время помнить, что надо быть добрым.
Будь не упрямым, а умным.
Не бойся, но и не храбрись.
Уклоняйся от спора.
Никогда не спорь, но и не соглашайся, если ты видишь,
                                          что это не так.
Ни о ком дурно не говори, ибо тот, кому ты дурно
говоришь о другом, – такой же.
Жизнь, как говорят, всему научит, но помни – надо быть
          смышленым учеником.
Не надейся на себя.
Не рассчитывай на других.
Ничего не жди.
Жди только смерть – она придет.

Evgeny Kropivnitsky

From '100 Tips for Myself'

Be humble, never get angry.
Always repent, as you are as sinful as anybody.
Keep in mind that you ought to be kind.
Don't be stubborn, be wise.
Don't be afraid, but don't boast of your bravery.
Dodge an argument.
Never argue, but don't agree with something that isn't true.
Don't badmouth anyone, for the one you speak to can be as vile
                                                    as the other.
They say life will teach you everything, but try to be a smart
            student.
Don't rely on yourself.
Don't count on the others.
Don't expect anything.
Wait only for death – it won't fail to come.

Полустертая Эпитафия

Здесь похоронен... (временно –
Кладбище ликвидируют.)
Во цвете лет... Безвременно...
(Тут, видимо, датируют.)
(И дальше крупно) – ОВ
(Должно быть, Иванов.)

Half-Erased Epitaph

Here lies... (temporarily –
The cemetery is being liquidated.)
In the prime of life... untimely...
(Here, apparently, the dates of birth and death.)
(And lower, in a larger print) – OV
(Must have been Ivanov.)

Объявление на Столбе

Продается
Белая коза –
Желтые глаза.
У Смирновых отдается
Дом в наем:
Есть хлевушка,
Погребушка –
Все при ем.

На столбушке
Всем на погляденье
Клеют объявления:
У Макарьевой старушки
Бочка есть,
Есть лаханка.
Так же дранка
Нова есть.

Lamppost Ads

For sale:
A she-goat, white
With yellow eyes.
The Smirnovs advertise
A house to let,
With a cattle-shed
And a cellar –
All in good shape.

Folks glue ads
To the lamppost
For everyone to see:
Old woman Makaryeva
Has a tun
And a wash-tub.
Also roof-tiles,
New but old-style.

* * *

Мне очень нравится, когда
Тепло и сыро. И когда
Лист прело пахнет. И когда
Даль в сизой дымке. И когда
Так грустно, тихо. И когда
Всё словно медлит. И когда
Везде туман, везде вода.

When...

I really like it when
It's warm and damp. And when
Leaves smell of must. And when
The horizon hides in a blue haze. And when
All is so sad, so quiet. And when
Life takes a pause. And when
There's fog everywhere, water everywhere.

Развод

Её муж сказал:
Она мне не нужна.
Он сказал:
Она обыкновенная –
Подводит глаза,
Пьёт водку, ест селёдку,
Курящая, как гулящая...
Ну и вот –
Нужен развод.

Divorce

Her husband said:
Don't need her.
He said:
She's ordinary:
Uses eyeliners,
Drinks vodka, eats herring,
A smoker, not far from a street-walker...
So this is what we've got:
A divorce sought.

Виктор Некипелов

Молитва Цветов

Коса прошла
по пойме луговой,
Коса прошла,
пока мы мирно спали.
Коса прошла
лавиной роковой,
И головы горячие упали.
Мы маленькие, робкие цветы,
Мы маленькие призрачные звуки,
Мы маленькие слуги Красоты,
Хоть красота не лечит наши муки.
Хоть красота цветет и на крови,
Хоть красота любые крепит своды,
Хоть красота, как дети без любви –
Была не раз зачата без свободы.
О дай нам Бог
однажды не стерпеть,
О дай нам Бог
постичь азы науки,
О дай нам Бог
сплести в тугую плеть
Безвольные, утонченные руки!

Victor Nekipelov

Flowers' Prayer

The scythe has cut
through the floodplain.
The scythe has cut through our meadows
while we were sleeping peacefully.
The scythe has cut through our meadows
like a fatal avalanche,
And some hot heads fell.
We are tiny timid flowers,
We are quiet ghostly sounds,
We are little servants of Beauty,
Even though Beauty won't ease our torment;
Even though Beauty feeds on blood;
Even though Beauty strengthens any vaults;
Even though Beauty, like unloved children,
often gets conceived amid the lack of freedom.
Oh Lord, grant us
days of non-endurance;
Oh Lord, grant us
comprehension of some science basics;
Oh Lord, let us
weave our delicate weak-willed hands
into a scourge!

Морская Прогулка

Какие у нас ветровые,
Косматые, дикие кони!
По сердцу – толчками – впервые,
Надежда уйти от погони.
От давней, навязчивой боли,
От вкрадчивой, ласковой скуки,
По ветру – две лилии воли –
Твои обнаженные руки!
Я знаю: мы близки, мы близки.
В каскадах сверкающей пыли –
Всё прочее напрочь забыто.
Мы тени? Мы души? Мы блики?
Сквозь толщу подводную чьи-то
Бегущие, зыбкие лики.
И соль оседает, как иней,
На гривы, на губы, на сети.
Мы двое – на первой, на синей,
Еще не остывшей планете.
Как чисто, как ладно, как гордо!
По сердцу – толчками – свобода!
И схвачено спазмою горло
От запаха ветра и йода.
А там, где сливаются тверди, –
Мощеная солнцем дорога
К чертогу ликующей смерти,
Известной под именем Бога.

Boat Trip

Horses of wind we've got,
These shaggy wild horses!
Pulsating in my heart for the first time, there's
A hope of getting away from the chase,
From the old meddlesome pain,
From creeping, caressing boredom.
Downwind, your uncovered arms,
Two lilies of volition!
I know: we're close, very close.
Everything else is left behind
In the cascades of sparkling dust.
Are we shadows? Or souls? Or maybe sparks?
Some shaky rippled faces show
Through the water's thickness.
And salt settles, like hoarfrost,
On lips, manes, and fishing nets.
The two of us are on the primal blue planet
That hasn't yet cooled down.
How clean it is, how harmonious, majestic!
Freedom is pulsating in my heart!
And there's a lump in my throat
From the smell of wind and iodine.
And there's a sun-paved road
Where the realms merge,
The road to the palace of jubilant death
That goes by the name of God.

Тишина

Дань разбит на шаги.
Тридцать тысяч шагов
От стены до стены...
    Тишина
Как сошедший с ума звездочет –
Я веду этот странный – кому же зачтется он, – счет...
    Тишина.
Говорил мне Конфуций
(А может, то был Эпикур?)
За бокалом вина,
Развалясь на циновке:
– Что-то, парень, ты хмур.
Не печалься!
Не надо бояться веков
И оков,
Старина!
Бойся только богов.
И долгов!
Ха-ха-ха!
    Тишина – это мудрость, – изрек он с бокалом вторым,
Все иное – пустяки.
Суета, наваждение, дым...

О, лукавый старик!
Я презрел твой недобрый совет.
Чепуха!
Ты философ, я только поэт.
Не бессмерться, а жизни ищу.
Не хочу в разгребатели книг...

– За вино я плачу, – он промолвил с ухмылкой и сник.
Растворился, исчез...
    Тишина.
    Ля бемоль...

Silence

The day is broken into steps,
Thirty thousand steps
From wall to wall...
    Silence
Is like a crazy stargazer:
I take a count, a strange one – who's going to check it?
    Silence.
Confucius said to me
Over a glass of wine
While lounging on a mat
(Or was it Epicurus?):
Why this doom and gloom, man?
Don't worry!
Don't be afraid of centuries
And shackles,
Old fella!
Only fear the gods
And debts!
Ha-ha!
    Silence is wisdom, he pontificated raising the second glass,
Everything else is nonsense.
Vanity, obsession, smoke...

O sly old man!
I rejected your unkind advice.
Such nonsense!
You're a philosopher, and I but a poet.
I don't seek immortality, but I yearn for a life.
I don't want to be a book-raker...

I'll pay for the wine, he said with a grin and wilted,
Dissolved in the air, vanished...
    Silence.
    The key of A-flat...

А еще ты сказал, что она – как лебяжье крыло.
Как... смакуя губами сравненье, добавил: барсучья
      нежнейшая кисть!..

Ерунда!
      Тишина – это боль.

Это бьющая в трюмы вода.
Это лампочки белый накал...
И зубное сверло...
Это крик изнутри, из зеркал,
Это черепа шепот – в висках:

      «Отрекись! Отрекись!»

Ах, какая гроза – среди ночи – рыданием в сны!
Вот... я знаю теперь,
Как понять выраженье
      «аккорд тишины»,
Это – черный шпицрутен.
Обрыв сумасшедшей струны.
Это ветка ночная, хлыстнувшая в кровь по лицу...

Не хочу тишины!
Никогда! Никому.
Ни врагу. Ни глупцу.
Не хочу ее даже тому –
      Подлецу.

And you also said that silence was like a swan's wing,
Like a badger's gentle paw, you added
    savouring the comparison's taste on your lips.

Nonsense!
    Silence is pain.

It's water battering the ship's hold.
It's the white heat inside an electric bulb...
A dental drill...
It's a scream from within, from the mirrors;
It's a whisper inside your skull that causes a temple pain:

    Renounce it! Renounce it!

Ah, what a thunderstorm in the middle of the night
    penetrating dreams like sobbing!
So... I know now
The meaning of the phrase
    'a chord of silence':
It's a black cane;
A broken crazy string;
A nightly branch that whips you across the face making you bleed...

I don't want silence!
Never! For anybody.
Neither for an enemy nor for a fool.
Don't even want it for that man,
    The villain.

Всеволод Некрасов

* * *

Молчу
Молчи

Молчу
Молчи

Чутьем
Чутьем

Течем
Течем

Я думал
Мы о чем молчим

А мы молчали
Вот о чем

Vsevolod Nekrasov

Untitled 1

I am silent
Keep silence

I am silent
Keep silence

By guess-work
By touch

We move on
We move further

I thought
We hushed something up

But we hushed up
This

* * *

надо же
и тишина между нами
мальчиками и девочками

кусты
столбы и луны
луны луны ну
не было войны

скажи ты

будто бы
а пусто
было

не было пусто

Untitled 2

picture this:
hushed silence dwells between us
between boys and girls

bushes
telegraph poles – and moons
many moons – as though
there was no war

one could say

as though
there was
only void

there wasn't

* * *

Стой

Чувствуй

Гордись

куда денешься

вот теперь и гордись

столица

и столица гордится

вечным памятником
великим нашим
начальникам

как они стучали
на нас

каким большим большим
Кулаком

Pride

Stop

Feel

Be proud

you have no place to hide

so be proud now

capital city –

our capital is proud too

of the eternal monument
to our great
leaders

how they banged
on their tables talking to us

banged on their tables with their big
BIG fists

* * *

Не люблю
Что я люблю
Но люблю
Что не люблю

Но что это я люблю
То что это я люблю
Это я не говорю
Что я это говорю

Love

I don't love
What I love
But I love
What I don't love

But what is it I love?
The fact that I love it
I am not saying
That I am saying that

* * *

вот кто
виноваты

разговоры разговоры
интеллигенты интеллигенты
чемберлены чемберлены
разгильдяи разгильдяи
инциденты инциденты
эпизоды эпизоды
экземпляры экземпляры
элементы элементы
симулянты
спекулянты
белофинны
контрабандисты
конкуренты конкуренты
интуристы интуристы
менделисты морганисты
формалисты
космополиты
мейерхольды мейерхольды
мандельштамы мандельштамы
буратины буратины
чебурашки чебурашки
интервенты интервенты
антиподы
оппоненты
супостаты
басурманы
виноваты
фантомасы
виноваты масоны

Who is to Blame?

They are
to blame:

talks, talks
eggheads, eggheads
Bohemians, Bohemians
incidents, incidents
episodes, episodes
specimens, specimens
elements, elements
simulators
speculators
Chamberlains, Chamberlains
White Guard
White Finns
smugglers, smugglers
rivals, rivals
foreign tourists
geneticists
formalists
cosmopolites
Meyerholds, Meyerholds
Mandelstams, Mandelstams
Fantomases, Fantomases
Pinocchi, Pinocchi
interventionists
invaders
antipodes
opponents
tyrants
infidels
they all are to blame
freemasons
to blame

Ры Никонова

* * *

Кареты в белом
Портреты в черном
Все слуги в синем
все так красивы
все – из России
все так смешны
Все так нарошно
все так заброшено
  так огорожено
  так огорошено
Все так кошмарно
все так несложно

Rea Nikonova

Simple

Ambulances in white
Portraits in black
All servants in blue
all are from Russia
all are so beautiful
all are so funny
everything is so deliberate
everything is so abandoned
     so fenced off
     so uprooted
Everything is so eerie
everything is so simple

* * *

Все идиоты в этом мире идиотов
И каждый идиот идет отдельно

Все патриоты в этом мире идиотов
и каждый идиот идет отдельно

И каждый идиот по-каждому живет

В этом мире
в этом мире
каждый – идиот

The World of Idiots

How many idiots in this world of idiots
each idiot performing solo

How many patriots in this world of idiots
each idiot performing solo

And each idiot is an idiot in his own way

In this world
in this world
each one is an idiot

Анти-новелла

Полное отсутствие действия

Никто ничего не делает
Никто нигде не находится
Никто ни к чему не стремится

Финал
Апофеоз тишины

Anti-Novella

Absolute absence of action

No one does anything
No one is present anywhere
No one seeks after anything

The grand finale
Triumph of stillness

* * *

Когда помру
я стану знаменитой
Я знаменитой
знаменитой
стану
стану
Я стану
стану
стану
стану знаменитой
Ах
знаменитой
знаменитой
стану
стану

Foretaste

When I pop off
I shall be famous
Famous
famous
I shall be
I shall
I know
I shall
I shall
I shall be famous
Ah
how famous
famous
famous
I shall be

* * *

Россия с исснеженным зубром!
Твоей заповедной золы
я запах храню
для неубранных
для сладостно помнящих дым

Russia

O Russia, with its snow-covered aurochs!
I keep the smell of your sacred ashes
for those unharvested
for those delighted to remember
the sweetest fumes

Григорий Подъяпольский

* * *

Вокс попули – вокс деи...
                   Но и боги,
Бывает, ошибаются.
                   И вот
Старушка тащит на костер для Гуса
Вязанку хвороста...
                   Ах, бедный Гус!
И бедная святая простота...

(Особенно, которая не очень…)

Grigory Podyapolsky

Vox populi

Vox populi, vox Dei...
>   But the gods too
Can be error-prone.
>   And so
An old woman drags a brushwood bundle
To the bonfire of the burning Jan Hus.
>   Alas, poor Hus!
Alas, the regrettable *sancta simplicitas...*

(Especially where it is less than holy...)

Отчаянье

Не мотыльков бесплодное сгоранье
И не тоска за письменным столом...
Отчаянье не двигало мирами,
И ничего еще не создало,
И никуда не отворило двери...

Отчаянье оставим тем, кто верил.

Despair

Nothing like moths' pointless burning
Or anguish at a writing desk...
Despair never set the world alight,
Or created worthy things,
Or opened the door to some nice place...

We'll leave despair to those who still believe.

Индийская философия

Бог совершенен – правду говорят,
И кроме Бога ничего не надо.
И бодрствуй Бог, все было бы олл райт,
Но Бог заснул...
А в это время Дьявол

Тяп-ляп – и создал мир.
Посредственный весьма.
Какой из Дьявола, помилуйте, работник?
Добро была бы цель, а то из озорства.
К тому ж еще спешил, не вкалывал добротно.

А мы расхлебывай, как попки, это все:
И шутки Дьявола, и тихий Божий сон...

Indian Philosophy

God is perfect – what they say is true,
And apart from him, nothing else is needed.
Were God awake, all would be in order,
But he fell asleep...
Meanwhile, the Devil

Did some sloppy job – and built the world,
A rather mediocre one.
What kind of worker is he anyway?
He had no goal and did things out of mischief.
Besides, he worked apace and didn't take the trouble.

And now we, like parrots, sort out all that:
The Devil's follies and God's undisturbed slumber...

Из цикла «Кабинет»

Кабинет был обширен, как я сказал.
Кабинет был почти как зал.
Но его половину (огромен столь)
Занимал
Генерал
Стол!

...Немного поэт, я стол любил
(У Цветаевой есть о том),
Но тут сперва: шириной с Сибирь,
А что это был стол – потом.

From 'The Office'

The office was extensive, I repeat.
The office was almost like a dancing hall.
But a table occupied (once and for all)
Half the room;
The table called
The General.

... A kind of poet, I adored that piece of furniture
(Tsvetaeva once wrote a similar fable) –
Its main feature was, ample as Siberia,
And, less important: it still was a table.

* * *

О-сень...
       Золотая о-сень.
Золотая...
        Голубая...
              – Се-рая.
Мне что-то горестно очень.
Верую,
Что зима будет
      (а это – точно),
И холодно
      (тоже факт),
И что эти последние грустные листочки
Со-всем облетят...

Autumn

Autumn...
      A golden autumn.
Golden...
       Blue...
            – Gre-e-e-y.
I'm somewhat sad today.
I believe
That winter won't fail to come
      (and that's certain)
And it will be a cold one
      (also a fact)
And that the last sad leaves
Will all fall down...

Генрих Сапгир

Умирающий Адонис

Я – Адонис
Я хромаю и кровь течет из бедра
Я корчусь – червяк на ладони
Не отворачивайся Природа будь добра
Я – сын твой Адонис

Меня погубила дура из бара
Обступили какие-то хмуро и серо
Я падаю – мне не дожить до утра
Мне дурно

Вот приближается рокот мотора
Меня освещает белая фара
Как твое имя парень?
Адонис
'Адонис? Латыш наверно или эстонец'

Я – Адонис
Я совсем из другого мира
Там апельсины роняет Флора
Там ожидает меня Венера
И о несчастье узнает скоро
Дикие вепри
Бродят на Кипре...

Ах ты бедняжка!
'Понял! он – итальяшка'

Genrikh Sapgir

Dying Adonis

I am Adonis
I am limping, my thighs are bleeding
I writhe like a worm on somebody's palm
Mother Nature, I beg thee, don't turn your back on me
I am your son Adonis

A stupid barmaid ruined me
Some gloomy figures beset me
I stumble, I won't live until morning
I am about to faint

Suddenly – roaring of a motor
A white shaft of light
'What's you name, lad?'
'Adonis'
'Adonis? Must be Latvian or Estonian'

I am Adonis
I came from a different world
Flora drops slow oranges there
Venus is waiting for me
And will soon learn about my misfortune
Wild boars are roaming
In Cyprus...

'Poor thing!
He's from Italy, I think.'

Я – Адонис!
Я чужой этим улицам и магазинам
Я чужой этим людям и трезвым и пьяным
Поездам телевизорам телефонам
Сигаретам газетам рассветам туманам

'Нет
Скорей
Это
Еврей'

Я – Адонис
Я сквозь дебри за вепрем бежал и дрожал
Меня ветки за пятки хватали пытали
Меня били! любили! хотели! потели!
Я любезен богине Венере
Я не здесь! Я не ваш! Я не верю!

Сумасшедший ясно
Но откуда он?
Неизвестно

Я – Адонис

I am Adonis
I am a stranger to these streets and shops
These telephones TV sets and bus stops
Cigarettes newspapers dawns and fogs
I have nothing in common with those folks...

'He sounds
like a Jew'
'He is one
I tell you'

I am Adonis
I was forcing my way through thickets
I was chasing a wild boar
Branches grasped me by my heels
I was sweating I was beaten I was loved I was wanted
Venus is fond of me
I don't belong here I am not one of you

'A half-wit, surely'
'But where does he come from?'
'No one knows.'

I am Adonis

Зло

в младенце сидело
Зло

оно сжимало
пухлые нежные кулачки
топотало
розовыми ножками
(все в перевязочках)
рот –
шире лица:
дай!
земля намазана небом –
толстый пирог
ешь – не хочу!..

но когда оставались
последние крохи
старик взвыл:
Боже мой! Боже!
меня сожрало
Зло

Evil

inside the baby
Evil was hiding

Evil clenched its
plump and tender fists
Evil tramped the floor
with its tiny pink feet
(all bandaged up)
out of Evil's mouth
as broad as its face:
give me this! give me that!
the land was spread with skies
like a thick pie:
appease your appetite!..

with only a few crumbles left
the old man
screamed:
Oh, my God!
Evil
has gobbled me up!

Роща

со всей своей зеленой тенью
с поросшими мохом голыми стволами
со всеми своими гладкими листочками и птицами
со всеми своими ползающими и бегающими
с грузином который порвал газету
и приспустив штаны сидит на корточках
быть может вся эта самшитовая роща –
одна вечно-зеленая трель соловья

Grove

with all its green shadows
with naked tree boles covered with moss
with all its birds and smooth leaves
with all that creep and run
with a Georgian man who has just torn a newspaper
lowered his pants and squatted down –
perhaps this boxwood grove is
an evergreen trill of a nightingale

Суд

Беседую как с другом,
С Богом.
Но верю лишь своим
Ногам.
Они несут меня, несут
На площадь –
На Великий Суд.
Что случилось?
Кого собираются вешать?
Отвечайте же скорее!
Говорят,
Казнят
Еврея.
Спрашиваю одного героя:
Неужели всех
Врачей? –
(Смех.)
Рабиновича?
Рабиновича.
А Гуревича?
И Гуревича.
И Петрова Ивана Петровича?
Покосился этот тип.
Холодный пот
Меня прошиб.
Ты сам, случайно,
Не сектант?

The Trial

I talk with God
as with a friend
but I only believe in my legs,
in the end.
They carry me, they bring me
to the square.
The Last Judgement is on there.
'What's happening?
Who are they going to hang?
Tell me!'
They say, they are
executing
a Jew.
'Not all the medical men,
by any chance?'
I address a man of courage.
(Laughter.)
'Rabinovich?'
Rabinovich!
 'And Gurevich?'
Surely, Gurevich!
'And Petrov Ivan Petrovich?'
The chap looks at me askance.
I grow cold with fear.
You are not far
from a dissident,
yeah?

Товарищи,
Интеллигент! –
Тут окончилась война,
И началась такая бойня,
Что даже Бог –
Мой лучший друг –
Никого не уберег.

У Бога есть один дефект:
Его смущает интеллект.

Look, lads,
an egghead!
That instant the war came to its end
and the butchery began,
killings without remorse.
Even God, my best friend,
couldn't save anyone from the worst.

God has a critical defect:
he is perplexed by intellect.

* * *

Тс-с
Слышите

И еще

И это

И там

И далеко-далеко

Sounds of Silence

Hark, hearer
can you hear it?

And this

And again

And there

And far, far away

Ян Сатуновский

* * *

В век сплошной электрификации
всем
всё
до лампочки.
Так что даже левые поэты
пишут
правые стихи.

Ian Satunovsky

Changing the Bulb

In the age
of total electrification
no one
cares a blinking damn.
And so left-wing poets
write
right-wing poems.

* * *

В некотором царстве,
в некотором государстве,
в белокаменной Москве
                              краснопролетарской
тридцать лет и три года
жили-проживали
старичок со старушкой в полуподвале.
А на тридцать четвертый год
                              случилось чудо:
в переулке,
где ютилась их лачуга,
точно вынутые из улья восковые соты,
от лесов освободился дом высотный.
И теперь старичок со старушкой,
проживающие в полуподвале,
за окошком видят Герб Союзный,
за который мы воевали.

A Basement Flat

In some kingdom,
in this realm,
in white-stone Moscow,
            red-proletarian,
in a basement flat
there lived
for thirty-three years
an old man and an old woman.
And in the course of the thirty-fourth year
                a miracle happened:
in the small alley
where their shack huddled
like a beeswax honeycomb extracted from the hive,
a skyscraper emerged from scaffolding.
And now the old man and the old woman,
who dwell in the basement, can see out the window
the State Emblem of the Soviet Union,
for which we fought a war.

* * *

Экспрессионизм-сионизм.
Импрессионизм-сионизм.
Но и в РЕАЛИЗМЕ, при желании,
обнаружат сговор с ИЗРАИЛЕМ.

If They So Desire

Expressionism is Zionism.
Impressionism is Zionism.
But even in REALISM, if they so desire,
they will discover a collusion with ISRAEL.

* * *

Ребенок рисунка:
вроде как машинально,
почти по ошибке
художник
нанес на холст
смертельный намек.

Almost by Mistake

A child of the drawing:
seemingly in a mechanical way,
almost by mistake
the artist
deposited a deadly allusion
onto the canvas.

* * *

              ...а, впрочем,
не всё ли нам равно – писать – свободным
или каким-нибудь еще – стихом
в концентрационном лагере...

Writing

                            ... but then
isn't it all the same to us – to write in free verse
or in some other kind of verse
in this concentration camp...

* * *

Я Мойша з Бердычева.
                   Я Мойзбер.
А, может быть, Райзман.
                   Гинцбург, может быть.
Я плюнул в лицо
                   оккупантским гадинам.
Меня закопали в глину заживо.
Я Вайнберг.
Я Вайнберг из Пятихатки.
Я Вайнберг.
                   За что меня расстреляли?
Я жид пархатый дерьмом напхатый.
Мне памятник стоит в Роттердаме.

A Bloody Yid

I am Moishe from Berdichiv.
                        I'm Moisber.
Or maybe Raizman.
                        Perhaps Ginsburg.
I spat in the faces
                   of the invading scum.
I was buried alive in clay.
I'm Weinberg.
I'm Weinberg from Pyatikhatka.
I'm Weinberg.
                Why did they shoot me?
I'm a bloody yid stuffed with shit.
A monument to me was erected in Rotterdam.

Михаил Соковнин

* * *

Вот вам и чудо:
из голубого пруда
торчит чертик.
Да,
на фантазию всюду
и всегда
нужна зацепка.
В данном случае –
щепка.

Mikhail Sokovnin

Fantasy

Here's a miracle for you:
a little devil
sticks out of the blue pond.
Yes,
to get fantasy
up and running
one always needs a lever.
In this case,
a sliver.

Лесовик

Н.С.Г.

Лесовик уставился на – солнце.
Будто понимает, что оно –
что оно с собою унесется
даже в землю, где всегда темно,
и что если не забудет солнца,
по закону солнца-колеса
он опять родится, как проснется,
и продлится
сон лесовика.

Woodsman

for NSG

The woodsman stares at the sun –
As though he just realised that it –
That it will be carried away, by itself,
Even as far as the land of constant darkness,
And also that, if he doesn't forget the sun,
he'll be born again as he wakes up
according to the law of the sun-wheel –
and the woodsman's dream
will linger.

* * *

Самовар.
Сеновал.
Лето перезимовал.
Осень – ветер,
осень – дождь...
Так и смерть переживешь.

Samovar

A samovar.
A hayloft.
...hibernated the whole summer.
Autumn is wind,
autumn is rain.
This way you'll survive your death.

* * *

Небо серое-серое.
Небо северное.
Мало перьев на сосне,
и сквозящая макушка
в небо просится.
Отчего она, кукушка,
по весне?
Отчего она не по осени?

A Northern Song

The sky is the greyest grey.
The sky is a northern one.
There're some feathers atop the pine,
and its drafty crown
strives for the sky.
Why is this cuckoo
in spring?
Why isn't it in autumn?

* * *

Заброшенные истины,
колодцы прежних дней.
Над травами когтистыми
пустые перстни пней.

Untitled

Abandoned truths,
wells from the days of old...
Above the clawed grass,
empty signet rings of stumps.

Сергей Стратановский

* * *

Ночью, в Набоков-отеле
        школьницу, полую Лолу
В номер на птицу-постель
        змей-господин завлечет
Змей о семи головах:
        первая жрет насекомых
Гонгорой бредит вторая
Третья целует в пупок,
        в полудетские груди Лолиту
Зверь о семи головах
Веки закрыла седьмая:
        молится Богу впотьмах

Sergey Stratanovsky

In the Nabokov Hotel

At night, in the Nabokov Hotel
Sir Serpent entices a school-girl,
      the hollow Lola, into his room
      and onto his bird-shaped bed.
Seven-headed Sir Serpent.
The first head gorges itself on insects,
The second is mad about Gongora,
The third kisses Lolita on her navel
      and childish breasts.
Seven-headed Sir Beast.
The last head has weighed its eyelids down
      to pray to some God in the dark.

Акула-кунсткамера

Вот акула-кунсткамера. В ней
Головы турок в спирту
Петр в железных ботфортах
Церберша ангальт-цербстская:
     в ноздрях сияют алмазы
В заднице блещет топаз
Рядом кленовый Пахом,
     ладан, церковное пенье
Пушкин на девке верхом,
     пишущий стихотворенье
Дивно бродить и смотреть
В многокамерной рыбе, правдивой как смерть

A Shark as a Cabinet of Curiosities

Inside a shark there is a Cabinet of Curiosities.
Watch these heads of Turks preserved
    in alcohol, Tzar Peter in his iron jackboots,
The Cerberus of Anhalt-Zerbst,
    diamonds shining in her nostrils
And a topaz sparkling in her arsehole.
The maple Pakhom sits beside her.
It smells of an incense, a choir is singing.
Pushkin is also there positioned on top
    of a whore and writing a poem.
I do like to stroll through these rooms
    looking round and holding my breath
In this spacious fish, truthful as death.

Левиафан

Чешуеглазый,
    с дрожащим Ионой во чреве
В недрах узилища рыбного,
    в тесноте кровокамеры хищной
Страшно и нечем дышать
    в государстве его биоклеток
В социуме телец
    кровяных
        под командой турбинного мозга

Скоро ль извергнешь назад
    поглощенных, заглоченных толпы?
Скоро ль нырнешь без возврата
    вниз, на библейское дно?

Leviathan

Scaly-eyed,
    it harbours trembling Jonah in its belly,
In the bowels of its fishy dungeon.
How scary it must be –
    choking in that cramped
Blood-coloured chamber
    of some predatory cellulate republic,
Suffocating in the community of blood corpuscles
    under the command of a turbine brain!

When will you disgorge what you have swallowed,
    those countless multitudes?
When will you dive back
    to the scriptural depths, forever?

Башня-библиотека

Башня до самого неба,
      башня-библиотека
Вьющихся лестниц извивы,
      фолианты в размер этажей
Хмель-виноградьем увитые
      с заржавленными замками
На шумерских цепях
Здесь чернокнижье цветущее –
      тайную мудрость Адама
Кто-то постигнет, вместит,
      и тогда остановится время
Ангел свернет небеса

The Library Tower

It's a library tower,
     and it pierces the sky.
Hop and vine twine around
Winding stairs and storey-sized volumes.
All the locks on Sumerian chains
     are rusting.
Black magic is blooming here,
     the secret wisdom of Adam.
Some day somebody will apprehend
     and master it –
And time will come to a halt,
An angel will furl the sky

Апокриф

Вирус, откуда-то появившийся
И в Адама вселившийся
   на террасе Эдемского сада
Вирус, боль вызывающий,
Сокрушающий чресла,
   кровь рушащий,
Вирус невидимый
И Адам пораженный
   уходит из райского сада
Сам уходит,
   на горькую землю труда

An Apocryphal Story

The virus that appeared from Goodness knows where
And made its home inside Adam
      on the terrace of the Garden of Eden –
The virus causing pain,
Crushing the loins,
      ruining the blood,
The invisible virus –
And Adam, staggering,
      leaves the wonders of Eden,
Of his own will descends he
      onto the bitter earth of labour

Кари Унксова

* * *

Вот засевает воду пепел снега
И крутятся потерянные чайки.
Апрель кончается. Совсем промерзли вербы
И раздраженно лязгают трамваи.
Фиалки облетают на ветру
В руках у смуглых косвенных цыганок.
Метро прибежищем и спертой теплотой
Воскресные раскручивает толпы.
Но дрогнет очередь за семенами
И в магазине крошечном «природа»
В углу, среди аквариумных монстров,
В суровых стружках теплятся цыплята.
И после кофе, сигарет и прочих
Аксессуаров напряженной ночи
Я, грешная, смиренно провожаю
Тебя на эскалатор, а сама
Иду на рынок по букет укропа.

April

Snow ashes sow the water,
And lost seagulls toss about overhead.
April is at its end. Willows are frozen stiff,
And trams clank in exasperation.
Violets held by swarthy quirky gypsies
Lose their petals to the wind.
The Metro, its stale warmth... It's a refuge,
It spins the Sunday crowds.
And in a tiny nature shop, where the queue
For seeds flinches every now and then,
Chickens dwell in the corner among the frugal
Wood shavings that keep them warm
Beside aquarium monsters.
And after coffee, cigarettes, and other
Accessories of a busy night
I, sinful, accompany you humbly
To the escalator, and then make my way
To the market, where I buy a tuff of dill.

* * *

Черные доски забора
Теплый вечер
Тихо тихо тихо
Выращивает грибы
Когда уснет
Можно пойти к озеру
Хвоя вздыхает
Впитывает влагу
На дороге валяются сучья
Усталое спит
Поломанное спит
Тут где-то водится рысь
Птицы притихли
Никого
Пустая купальня
Пустые облупленные кабинки
Пацифики секс и мат
Пионерские лагеря опустели
Такая недвижная
Такая черная
Никаких отражений
Треск мотоцикла

Evening

Black fence boards
A warm evening
Falls asleep
Grows mushrooms
Quietly quietly quietly
One can go to the lake shore
Pine needles sigh
Absorb moisture
There are boughs lying on the road
All the tired asleep
All the broken asleep
There's a lynx on a prowl somewhere
Birds fall silent
No one around
An empty bath
Empty flaky cubicles
Peace and sex symbols, swear words
Pioneer camps all empty
So motionless
So black
No reflections
Just a motorbike crackle-and-pop

* * *

Ты слишком ДА
Смотри как ты идешь
Ты слишком пряди очи губы руки
Красы неведомой
И вот зане – не помнит
Никто тебя
К фиалке обратясь
Тут связь времен
Яснее
Запах тише
Настойчивей
И как-то обратим
Им можно пряники
Платок или водицу
Кто видел плод
У розы на устах
Кто горечь одиночества измерил?

Too Much

You're too much of a YES
Watch your steps
You're too much of your eyes tresses lips hands
Of your mysterious beauty
And so it is – no one remembers
Who you are
Look at the violet
Here the connection of times is
Clearer
The smell subtler
More persistent
And even reversible
It can be used for gingerbread
A handkerchief or toilet water
Who could foresee a fruit
On the lips of a rose?
Who measured the bitterness of seclusion?

* * *

На горе Лу
Дождь и туман
В реке Че
Высокая вода
Я знал что мне
Не найти покоя
Пока я вновь
Не вернусь сюда
И вот я вернулся.
Ничего особенного
На горе Лу
Дождь и туман
В реке Че
Высокая вода.

Zen

Rain and fog
Over Mount Lou
High water
In the river Che
I knew there wouldn't be
Peace for me
Until I
Come back here
And so I'm back.
Nothing special
Rain and fog
Over Mount Lou
High water
In the river Che.

Грачи Улетели

И незаметно улетают
Из лета громкие грачи...
Еще берез неистов смерч
И металлических осин
Не прикоснулся медный призвук
А вот – крылом проводит грач
Черту последнюю – на север
С холодным воздухом уплыв
С ближайшим двинувшись циклоном
А лес беспомощным циклопом
Смиряет мощный свой порыв
К движению. Как грозы редки
Но нет, все правильно. Лететь
И надо, летние щедроты
Меняя древним перелетом
На скупость тающей реки.

The Departure of Rooks

And so they fly quietly, these
Loud rooks, away from this summer.
Still here, the birch tornado frenzy
And the metallic aspens
Untouched by copper sounds.
And now a rook's wing draws
The final line and floats away
To northern lands in a cold air stream
Or with the nearest cyclone.
And the forest, like a helpless Cyclops,
Gives up its powerful impulse
To move. How rare are thunderstorms...
But no, all is in order. So there's a need
To fly in an old-fashioned manner
Exchanging summer bounties
For the melting river's avarice.

Biographical Notes

The Poets

Gennady Aigi (1934–2006) was born in the Chuvash Republic, and lived in Moscow. His translations of French poetry into the Chuvash language brought him recognition at the beginning of his career as a writer. However, his unusual work was not welcomed in Russian periodicals and publishing houses. Some of his poems were circulating in samizdat publications. After perestroika, he published many critically acclaimed books of his poetry in Russian and Chuvash, as well as numerous essays and translations. His poems were translated into many languages. A book of his poems in French translation entitled *Veronica's Notebook* was published in Paris in 1984. Peter France of Edinburgh published two books of his translations from Aigi into English, much appreciated. Aigi was awarded the Golden Wreath of Struga (Macedonia), the French Academy Translators' Award and the Andrey Belyi Prize for Poetry (1987). In 2000, he was awarded the first ever Boris Pasternak Prize for Poetry.

Yuri Aikhenvald (1928–1993) was born and lived in Moscow; the grandson of the philosopher Yuli Aikhenvald deported from Soviet Russia in 1922. His father, an economist and a friend of both Leon Trotsky and Nikolai Bukharin, was arrested in 1933, mother in 1938; father was executed in 1941. He started to write poetry in 1944, and was a member of the group that also had Naum Korzhavin and Sergey Yesenin's son Alexander Volpin among its members. In 1947, he began studying the Russian language and literature at the Moscow Pedagogical Institute. In 1949, he was arrested for anti-Soviet propaganda and exiled to Karaganda for ten years; in 1951, he was re-arrested and later held in a psychiatric hospital. Released in 1955, he graduated from the university, worked as a secondary-school teacher and, from 1957, published his poems in local periodicals. In 1960, he was put under the KGB surveillance. In 1968, he signed a letter protesting against the Yuri Galanskov and Alexander Ginsburg show trial and was subsequently fired from his teaching job. Since then, he worked as a full-time writer and literary translator. In 1975, he was briefly detained by the KGB and suffered a heart attack while being questioned. He had a heart condition ever since. Collections of his poems and prose appeared abroad, in Munich and New York, in the 1970s. Since 1987, a few of his books, including two poetry collections, were published in Russia.

Yuli Daniel was born in 1925 in Moscow, the son of the Jewish writer Mark Daniel. He fought in the World War Two, was wounded and had disability ever since. After graduation from the Moscow Regional Pedagogical Institute, where he studied the Russian language and literature, he worked as a school teacher. He translated poetry from foreign languages, and got a number of his translations published. He also wrote fiction. His short novel titled *Escape* was brought out by Detgiz Publishers and subsequently banned from sales. His novellas titled *Hands, The Man from Minapa, Moscow Speaking,* and *Atonement* were published in the West under the pseudonym Nikolai Arzhak. In September 1965 he was arrested on charges of 'anti-Soviet activity' and subsequently sentenced, along with the fellow writer Andrey Sinyavsky, to five years in a maximum-security concentration camp. He remained in prisons and concentration camps until September 1970. In 1971, his collection entitled *Poems from Captivity* was published in Amsterdam by the Herzen Foundation. He refused to emigrate, and died in Moscow in 1988.

Vladimir Earle (pen name of Vladimir Gorbunov) was born in St. Petersburg in 1947. Having worked as a fireman, a laboratory assistant and a watchman, he now works as a librarian. He started writing poetry in 1962 as a fifteen-year-old. In a few years' time he became a member of the so-called Helenooct group of young poets that existed between 1966 and 1971. His poems were widely published in samizdat and in the Western Russian-language magazines. Since the years of perestroika he has published three critically acclaimed collections of his rather experimental poetry, *Helenooctism* (1993), *The Grass, the Grass* (1995), *The Book of King* (2009), *Yesterday and The Day After Tomorrow* (2012), as well as a book of non-fiction, *In Search of the Lost Xeif* (1999), as well as many essays on the Russian literature of the twentieth century. A volume of his *Collected Poems* appeared in Saint-Petersburg in 2015. Among the authors he has translated into Russian are Samuel Beckett and Franz Kafka. He was awarded the Andrey Belyi Prize for Poetry (1986) and the David Burliuk Prize for life-long commitment to experimental poetry (1991).

Yuri Galanskov was born in 1939 in Moscow. He studied history at Moscow State University, but was expelled for voicing unorthodox political opinions. He then worked at the State Literary Museum in Moscow, and continued his studies of history, this time at the History and Archives Institute. He took part in poetry readings at the Mayakovsky monument in Moscow, where he recited, among others, his poem *The Human Manifesto*. In 1961, he edited the samizdat almanac titled *Phoenix,* which was one of the first samizdat publications in Soviet Russia. He tried to establish a pacifist association, and drafted its programme and a manifesto. In December 1965, he was one of the organisers of a demonstration in Pushkin Square in Moscow, after which he was detained for several months in a psychiatric hospital. In 1966, he joined the NTS (the National Alliance of Russian Solidarists), a Russian anti-communist organization. In January 1967, he was arrested and spent a year in Lefortovo Jail while being under investigation for publishing a literary almanac without the authorities' permission. The following year he, alongside three other dissidents, was tried in the so-called Trial of Four and sentenced to seven years in maximum-security camps, which caused protests in Russia and around the world. He was sent to a Mordovian camp, where he went on hunger strike several times and exposed abuses of human rights by the camp administration. Hard labour and systematic malnutrition had a detrimental effect on him; nevertheless he refused to submit a request for pardon, as this meant an admission of guilt. In October 1972, he underwent surgery in the camp hospital for perforated ulcer; qualified doctors were not allowed to operate on him, and so he was operated on by a fellow inmate, a medic but not a surgeon. He died of sepsis shortly after the operation.

Natalia Gorbanevskaya was born in 1936 in Moscow. She studied Russian literature first at Moscow State University, from which she was expelled in 1957 for dissident activities, and later at Leningrad State University, from which she graduated in 1964. A few of her poems made their way to the local periodicals, although most of them were circulating in samizdat and appeared in émigré publications. She also translated Polish literature. A civil-rights activist, she was first arrested in 1956 for being a member of a dissident group that protested against the Soviet invasion of Hungary. Later she was one of the founders and the first editor of *A Chronicle of Current Events* (1968–1982). On 25 August 1968, with seven others, she took part in the Red Square protests against the Soviet invasion of Czechoslovakia. In 1970, a Soviet court sentenced her to incarceration in a psychiatric hospital. She was released from the Kazan Special Psychiatric Hospital in 1972, and published an article about the abuse of psychiatry, which was weaponised against the dissidents in Soviet Russia. She emigrated from the USSR in 1975, settling in Paris, France, where she became a co-editor of *Continent* magazine and *Russkaya Mysl* newspaper. She also co-organised some of the Amnesty International events. From 1999, she co-edited the Russian edition of *Nowaja Polsza,* a magazine of Polish culture and literature, and later became a citizen of Poland. Since late 1990s, fifteen of her books of poetry and prose were published in Russia. In 2010, she was the recipient of the Russian Prize for poetry. English translations of her poetry made by Daniel Weissbort were published in England by Carcanet in 1972 and reprinted several times. She died in 2013 in Paris.

Igor Kholin (1920–1999) was born and lived in Moscow. In his youth, he was employed as a waiter, then joined the Russian Army, fought in World War II, was wounded, and retired when the war ended. At the beginning of the 1950s he became a member of the now famous Lianozovo group of poets and painters. Under the Communists, his poems appeared only in émigré magazines, such as *Strelets/The Archer* and *Tretya Volna/Third Wave*. In 1989, his first poetry book entitled *Poems with Dedications* was published in Paris in Russian and subsequently reprinted in Moscow. His next collection appeared in 1995. At the end of the 1990s, he published a number of his short stories. After his death in 1999, an ample volume of his *Collected Poems* appeared in Moscow, followed by another big volume, this time of his *Collected Stories*.

Viktor Krivulin (1944–2001) was born in Krasnodon, Ukraine. From 1947 he lived in St. Petersburg. He was educated at Leningrad State University, where he studied Russian and Italian literature. In the 1970s, he was closely associated with two of the Russian samizdat magazines, 37 and Severnaya Pochta/Northern Post, where he published his poems and essays. He belonged to the so-called New Leningrad school of poetry, which also included Joseph Brodsky, Elena Shvarts and Sergey Stratanovsky. After perestroika, he became involved in politics, and was at the head of the St. Petersburg branch of Democratic Russia, the pro-democracy political party. Among his critically acclaimed collections are *A Concert of Requests* (1993), *Borderland* (1994), *Bathing in Jordan* (1998), and *Poems of the Jubilee Year* (2001). His poems have been translated into many European languages. In 1978, he was awarded the first ever Andrey Belyi Prize for Poetry.

Yevgeny Kropivnitsky (1893–1979) was a Moscow poet, essayist, and artist. He started his career as a composer, and later, in the 1920s, became an artist. He started writing poetry in 1909, and by early 1930s became an accomplished poet. Since early 1950s his poetry was available in samizdat. He wrote about life in the suburbs of big Russian cities, and called himself 'the poet of the suburbs.' In mid-1950s his disciples formed the now famous Lianozovo group of poets and artists, of which he was an informal leader. His wife, son, daughter and a grandson were artists. In 1963, he was accused of being a 'formalist' and expelled from The Artists' Union. In 1977, his first collection of poems was published in Paris in the original Russian. Two posthumous books of his poetry were published in Moscow: *Earthly Comfort* (1989) and *Selected Poems* (2004). Some of his innovative flash fiction pieces were anthologised on several occasions, but most of them are considered to be lost.

Victor Nekipelov (1928–1989) was born in Harbin, China, into a Russian family of railway workers. In 1937, he and his mother came to the Soviet Union. In 1939, his mother was arrested and died in prison. In 1950, he graduated from the Military and Medical College in Omsk; in 1960, from the Kharkiv Medical Institute in Ukraine. After graduation, he worked as a pharmaceutical chemist in Ukraine. In 1966, his first collection of poems entitled *Between Mars and Venus* was published in Uzhgorod, Ukraine. His later work only appeared in samizdat. In 1970 he lost his job due to his involvement in the dissident movement; he moved to Vladimir, where he again worked as a pharmaceutical chemist. In 1973, he was arrested and later sentenced to two-year imprisonment for anti-Soviet propaganda. After his release in 1975, he published numerous articles on the abuses of human rights in the USSR, both in samizdat and in the West. In 1977, he became a member of the Moscow Helsinki Human Rights Watch Group. His book about weaponising psychiatry against the dissidents in Soviet Union titled *The Institute of Fools* was published in 1980 in New York, in English translation. In June 1980 he was sentenced to seven years' imprisonment in a maximum-security labour camp. Released in 1987, he emigrated to France. His health deteriorated during his ordeal in the camp, and he died in 1989. A book of his *Selected Poems* was published in 1992 in Boston, in the original Russian.

Vsevolod Nekrasov (1934–2009) was born and lived in Moscow. He was a member of the now famous Lianozovo group of poets and painters. Under the Communists, he was a samizdat poet, without permission to publish his work openly. His poems appeared in unofficial Russian magazines, including *37*. Since 1989, three collections of his poetry, much appreciated, were published in Moscow. These books entitled *Poems from a Magazine* (1989), *Inquiry* (1991) and *Fair and Less than Fair* (1996) were followed by the Novosibirsk publication of his *Selected Poems* (2002) and *Poems 1956–1983* (Vologda, 2012). *Ein Deutsche Buch*, a book of his essays translated into German, appeared in Bochum in 2002. His poems have been translated into several other European languages.

Rea Nikonova (pen name of Anna Tarshis, 1942–2014) was born in Sverdlovsk, lived for many years in Yeisk in southern Russia, and then in Kiel, Germany. She started writing poetry at the end of the 1950s, and later edited several samizdat magazines. Her rather experimental work was first published in samizdat and in the Western Russian-language magazines, before it began to appear in Russian periodicals in the 1990s. Her first collection of texts entitled *An Epigraph to Emptiness* was published in Moscow in 1997. She later had poetry books published in Germany, Canada and the U.S.A. *The Pared-Down Log of Poetry*, a volume of her new and collected poems, was published in 2002 in Spain. Gerald Janecek of Kentucky translated a number of her poems into English, and his translations have been widely anthologised. She won the Andrey Bely Poetry Prize and the David Burliuk Prize for life-long commitment to experimental poetry.

Grigory Podyapolsky (1926–1976) was born in Tashkent, Uzbekistan. In 1949, he graduated from the Moscow Institute of Petrochemical and Gas Industry and later worked as a researcher. In early 1960s, he published his poems in samizdat. A collection of his poems titled *The Golden Age* appeared in Germany in 1974. Since 1965, he was a human-rights activist; in 1969, became a co-founder of the Action Group for the Defence of Human Rights in the USSR; in 1972, a co-founder of the Human Rights Committee (with Andrey Sakharov). He lost his job in 1970 due to his involvement in the dissident movement. In 1973, he was sent to psychiatric evaluation in an attempt to confine him to an asylum, which failed due to the public resonance after this information was published in the West. In 1976, he was exiled to Saratov, where he soon died of a stroke. A posthumous collection of his poems titled *Of the Time and Myself* was published in Germany in 1978. In Russia, a volume of his poems and essays titled *The Golden Age That Never Was* was published in 2003.

Genrikh Sapgir (1928–1999) was born in Biysk, and lived in Moscow from his early childhood. He was a member of the now famous Lianozovo group of poets and painters. From 1959 he published poetry for children. As for his other poems, they only appeared in émigré magazines, such as *The Continent* and *Strelets/The Archer*. Since 1989 his poetry, short stories, plays and novels have been widely published in Russia. He represented Russia at numerous international festivals of poetry, and his work has been published in translation throughout the world. Three volumes of his *Collected Poems* appeared at the end of the 1990s. The English translation of his *Psalms* by Jim Kates of New Hampshire has been published in book form by Cold Hub Press in 2012. Sapgir was the recipient of various awards including the Pushkin Prize for poetry.

Ian Satunovsky (pen name of Yakov Satunovsky, 1913–1982) was born in Dnipro, Ukraine, and moved to Moscow as a teenager to study in a college. In 1931 he returned to Dnipro to study physical chemistry at Dnepropetrovsk State University, from which he graduated in 1938. He served in the Russian army from 1939 until the end of World War II. Having come back from the war, he settled in Electrostal near Moscow, where he worked as an engineer. He was close to the poets of the Lianozovo Group, and published fourteen books of his poetry for children. From the mid-1970s he published his poetic miniatures in émigré magazines. He printed seven copies of his *Selected Poems* on his home typewriter; they were bound as three volumes. Four critically acclaimed collections of his poems were published in Moscow posthumously, the latest being *Poems and Prose to Go with Them* (2012).

Mikhail Sokovnin (1938–1975) was born and lived in Moscow. A graduate of the Russian Literature department of Moscow State Pedagogical University, he worked as a tour-guide in a number of Moscow art museums. His poems, prose and translations from Alfred Tennison weren't published during his lifetime, but some of them were circulating in samizdat publications. The first posthumous publication occurred in 1978 in Paris. In the 1990s his poems began to appear in Russian periodicals. His first posthumous collection, *Discomposed Type,* appeared in 1995; his second, *Prose and Poetry,* in 2012.

Sergey Stratanovsky was born in 1944 in St. Petersburg. Having studied philology at St. Petersburg University, he has since worked as a librarian. He started writing poetry at the end of the 1960s; his poems have been published first in samizdat and in the Western Russian-language magazines. He belonged to the so-called New Leningrad School of poetry, which also included Joseph Brodsky, Elena Shvarts and Viktor Krivulin. In the 1970s, he edited a few samizdat magazines. His first collection entitled simply *Poems* was published in St. Petersburg in 1993. Ten critically acclaimed books of his poems followed more recently, two latest being *Dissonant Polyphony* (2016) and *Izbornik: Selected Poems 1968–2018*. In 2019, he was the recipient of the Parabola Prize from the Andrey Voznesensky Foundation.

Kari Unksova (1941–1983) was born in Almaty, Kazakhstan into a family of geologists from Leningrad. In 1945, the family returned to their home city. In 1965, she graduated from Leningrad State University, where she studied geology. By then, she had written quite a number of poems and became a member of the poetic group that also included Joseph Brodsky and Anri Volokhonsky. She was first published in Estonia, and later, in 1974, in a Russian literary magazine. In 1980, she served six months in prison in connection with her work on the samizdat feminist journal, which appeared in France without Soviet permission in September 1979. The other co-editors were pressed out of the country and subsequently emigrated. She was rearrested and sentenced to fifteen days in prison on an absurd charge of assaulting police officers. Upon release she was offered an exit visa, and was told she could leave the country with her husband and children, aged 8 and 17. On 3rd June 1983, when she was about to emigrate, she was hit and killed by a KGB surveillance car. Her sister Marina who accompanied her was also hit and injured, but survived. A samizdat edition of her poetry circulated in Leningrad posthumously. In 1985, a collection of her poems, smuggled out of the USSR by friends, was published in Tel-Aviv. In 2009, a book of her poems and essays edited by her sister was published in St. Petersburg.

The Translator

Anatoly Kudryavitsky was born in 1954 in Moscow, of mixed Polish/Irish parentage. In the late 1970s he was involved in the dissident movement, briefly detained in 1979 but released due to the lack of evidence; from 1979 until 1989 he was blacklisted. In the 1980s, he worked as a researcher; later, he worked as a journalist, a creative writing tutor, an editor, and a literary translator. His poems and short stories first appeared in Russian periodicals in 1989. Since 1999, he has been living in Dublin, Ireland. He writes poetry in both English and Russian and fiction in Russian. He is the author of five collections of his English-language poetry, the latest being *The Two-Headed Man and the Paper Life* (MadHat Press, USA, 2019), which has also been published in translation into Romanian. He has edited and translated into English four bilingual anthologies of contemporary German, Ukrainian and Russian poetry, with Dedalus Press (Ireland) and Glagoslav Publications (UK). He has also published eight collections of his poetry in Russian, the latest two being *The Book of Gimmicks: Selected Prose Poems* (Yevgeny Stepanov Press, 2017) and *Outlines* (Free Poetry, 2020), as well as three novels, including *The Flying Dutchman* (Text Publishers, 2013; second edition: Eksmo Books, 2019; English translation: Glagoslav, 2018). He was the recipient of the Mihai Eminescu Academy Award for Poetry (Romania, 2017) and the Maria Edgeworth Poetry Prize (Ireland, 2003), as well as of multiple international awards for his English-language haiku.

Acknowledgements

Grateful acknowledgement is made to the editors of the following, in which a number of these translations, or versions of them, originally appeared: *Cyphers, Hayden's Ferry Review, Poetry Ireland Review, The SHOp, A Night in the Nabokov Hotel* (Dedalus Press, 2006), *Mirror Sand* (Glagoslav Publications, 2018).

Some of these poems, in English translation, were first broadcast on RTÉ Radio 1.

Every effort has been made to trace the holders of the copyright to the works by Yuli Daniel, Yuri Galanskov, Yevgeny Kropivnitsky, Victor Nekipelov, and Grigory Podyapolsky, and to obtain permissions to reproduce their works. Please do get in touch with any enquiries or any information relating to their poems or the rights holders.